1001
Animal
Quacker
Jokes

Robinson Children's Books

1001 Animal Quacker Jokes

Compiled by Jasmine Birtles

Illustrated by David Mostyn

Robinson Publishing Ltd
7 Kensington Church Court
London W8 4SP

First published in the UK by Robinson Children's Books,
an imprint of Robinson Publishing Ltd, 1998

A copy of the British Library Cataloguing in Publication
Data for this title is available from the British Library.

ISBN 1 85487 630 9

Printed and bound in the EC

10 9 8 7 6 5 4 3 2 1

CONTENTS

INTRODUCTION

Welcome to the finest collection of animal jokes around! In here you will find jokes about elephants, cows, tigers, cats, fish, dogs, giraffes, and gnats. You'll have the laugh of a lifetime with funny stories about kangaroo "hoperations," angora goat and warthog limericks, and animal insults for all occasions...in fact, there are enough jokes here to keep you chuckling for months. Reading this book will change your whole view of the animal world. It will also make you the most popular person in school and at home. So go on, impress your teacher with your second to none knowledge of wildlife...

...Why do elephants have such big trunks?
They have to travel all the way from Africa.

Show off your real understanding of cats...

...Why was the cat so small?
It only drank condensed milk.

Learn about the mental capacities of dogs...

...How can you tell if you have a stupid dog?
It chases parked cars.

and pick up all sorts of useful tips, like

How do you take a pig to hospital?
By hambulance.

By the end of the book you will be ready to make up your own animal jokes. Test them on your friends – they'll either love you or hate you!

Elephants

Did you know that the country with the most elephants is Tanzania in Africa? It has nearly 74,000 elephants. Elephants can sense if others are in pain or distress – even if the others are humans. A large elephant can produce as much heat as 30 people which is why African elephants have such large ears – to cool themselves on hot days. But do you know the best way to catch an elephant? Act like a nut and he'll follow you anywhere!

Why didn't the elephant cross the road?
Because he didn't want to be mistaken for a chicken.

What do you give an elephant with big feet?
Big flippers.

What is gray, has wings, a magic wand and a trunk?
The tusk fairy.

What do you call an elephant that is just three feet high?
Trunkated.

Why do elephants have such big trunks?
They have to travel all the way from Africa.

What's worse than an elephant on waterskis?
A porcupine on a rubber life raft.

How do you know when an elephant is about to charge?
He takes out his credit cards.

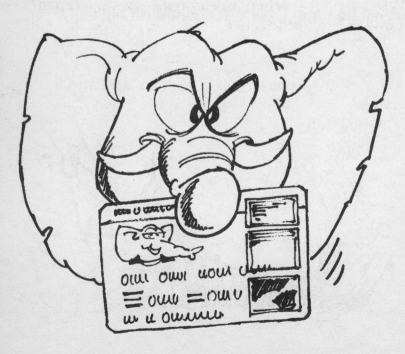

What do you get if you cross an elephant and a canary?
A messy cage.

How do you know if an elephant's come round for tea?
His tricycle's parked outside.

Why does an elephant have cracks between his toes?
So that he has somewhere to keep his cinema ticket.

What time is it when an elephant sits on a fence?
Time to mend the fence.

Why are elephants gray?
So they can't be mistaken for strawberries.

How do you know when there's an elephant
under your bed?
Your nose touches the ceiling.

What do you give a seasick elephant?
Plenty of room.

Why do elephants drink?
To forget.

Where did the flying elephant land?
At the earport.

Why did the elephant paint himself in rainbow colors?
Because he wanted to hide in the crayon box.

How does an elephant get down from a tree?
Sits on a leaf and waits for autumn.

How do you know if there's an elephant in your bed?
By the "E" on his pyjamas.

What is big and gray and protects you from the rain?
An umbrellaphant.

Why did the big game hunter give up hunting elephants?
He got tired of carrying around the decoys.

What is yellow on the outside, gray on the inside and has a good memory?
An elephant omelette.

How do you stop an elephant from going through the eye of a needle?
Tie a knot in his tail.

What do you call a dead elephant?
Nothing, he can't hear you.

Why do elephants live in zoos?
It's cheaper than renting a house.

Why is an elephant big, gray and wrinkled?
Because if it were small, yellow and feathery it
would be a canary.

What do elephants play when they are in the
car?
Squash.

What do you get when you cross an elephant with a computer?
A 5,000 pound know-it-all.

Why did the elephant leave the circus?
He was sick of working for peanuts.

Why can't an elephant ride a bicycle?
Because he doesn't have a thumb to reach the bell.

What is big and gray and lives in a Scottish lake?
Nessie the elephant.

How do you get rid of a white elephant?
Put it in a jumbo sale.

How do you get six elephants in a matchbox?
Take the matches out first.

What do you give a nervous elephant?
Trunquilizers.

How do you know if an elephant has been in your bed?
It's full of peanut shells.

Why do elephants lie down?
They can't lie up.

What is gray, has four legs and a trunk?
A mouse going on holiday.

What do you get if you cross an elephant with a mouse?
Enormous holes in the skirting board.

Why did the elephant paint his head yellow?
To see if blondes have more fun.

What is big, gray and loves curry?
An Indian elephant.

Which side of an elephant has the most skin?
The outside.

What's big, wrinkled and green?
An unripe elephant.

What did the grape say when the elephant trod
on it?
Nothing, he just let out a little wine.

What's big, gray, very heavy and wears glass slippers?
Cinderellaphant.

How many giraffes can you get in a car?
Four – two in the front and two in the back.

How many elephants can you get in a car?
None, it's full of giraffes.

Why did the elephant wear red shoes?
His blue ones were in the wash.

Why do elephants have trunks?
Because they'd look silly with handbags.

Why do elephants like rolling in mud?
Because they think it's slick.

Where does an elephant go on holiday?
Tuscany.

Why are elephants big, gray and wrinkly?
Because if they were small, round and white
they would be aspirins.

Why did the elephant sit on the piano?
Because he wanted to play squash.

Is it hard to bury a dead elephant?
Yes, it's a huge undertaking.

What has two tails, two trunks and five legs?
An elephant with spare parts.

Why do elephants have trunks?
So they have somewhere to hide.

What's a jumbo jet?
A flying elephant.

What was the elephant doing on the freeway?
About five miles per hour.

What should you do if an elephant charges?
Pay and run.

Where are elephants found?
They're so big they're hardly ever lost.

Why do elephants paint their feet yellow?
So that they can float in custard.

Why did the elephant cross the road?
Because it was the chicken's day off.

Why do elephants have wrinkles?
Have you ever tried ironing one?

What do you get if you cross an elephant with a
loaf of bread.
A sandwich that will never forget.

What's big, heavy and gray and has 16 wheels?
An elephant on roller-skates.

What do elephants sing at Christmas?
Jungle bells.

What's the difference between an elephant and a fly?
Quite a lot really.

What do you get if you cross an elephant with a kangaroo?
Great big holes all over Australia.

What's the biggest ant in the world?
An eleph-ant.

What happened to the elephant when he drank too much?
He got trunk.

What do you call the stupidest elephant in the world?
Dumbo.

What do you get if an elephant sits on your best friend?
A flat mate.

What do you get if an elephant sits on your piano?
A flat note.

How do elephants get power?
With ele-tricity.

Why do elephants paint their ears green and their trunks red?
So that they can hide in rhubarb patches.

What do elephants wear on their legs?
Elepants.

What's the difference between an elephant and a biscuit?
You can dip your biscuit in your tea.

How do you know if an elephant's been in your fridge?
There are footprints in the butter.

How do elephants hide?
They paint their toenails red and hide in rose
bushes.

What would you say if you saw a herd of
elephants coming over the hill?
"Oh look, there's a herd of elephants coming
over the hill."

What would you say if you saw a herd of
elephants wearing sunglasses coming over the
hill?
Nothing – you wouldn't recognize them.

Why shouldn't you dance with an elephant?
Because you'd end up with flat feet.

Why should you always tell an elephant the date of your birthday?
Because an elephant never forgets.

Why do elephants live in the jungle?
Because they're too big to live in a house.

How do you get an elephant into a car.
Open the door.

Why did the elephant have big ears?
Because Noddy wouldn't pay the ransom.

What do you call an elephant in a phone box?
Stuck.

What's big, red and hides behind a bush?
An embarrassed elephant.

What does it mean if you have an elephant in
your fridge?
He slept over, after the great party you had last
night.

Cat got your tongue?

Do you have a cat at home? A cat is the most popular pet of all in the United States and it's the second most popular in Britain. The most popular cat names are Sooty, Tigger and Tiger. The Manx cat is unusual because it doesn't have a tail and the fishing cat of India has slightly webbed paws to flip fish out of the water to eat. But where can you find the best selection of cats? In a catalogue of course.

What looks like half a cat?
The other half.

What happened when the cat ate a ball of wool?
She had mittens.

What do you get if you cross a cat with a parrot?
A carrot.

How do cats eat spaghetti?
Same as everyone else – they put it in their mouths.

What is a French cat's favorite pudding?
Chocolate mousse.

What do cat actors say on stage?
"Tabby or not tabby."

What did the cat say when he lost all his money?
I'm paw.

How do you know if your cat's got a bad cold?
He has cat-arrh.

How do you know if your cat has eaten a duckling?
She's got that down in the mouth look.

What do you get if you cross a cat with a gorilla?
An animal that will put *you* out at night.

What do you do with a Blue Burmese?
Try and cheer her up a bit.

What is the cat's favorite TV show?
The Evening Mews.

What's worse than raining cats and dogs?
Hailing taxi cabs.

How is cat food sold?
Usually purr can.

What noise does a cat make going down the
highway?
Miaoooooooooooooooooooooooooow.

What do you get if you cross a cat with a canary?
Shredded tweet.

What's the unluckiest kind of cat to have?
A catastrophe.

What do you get if you cross a cat with a tree?
A cat-a-log.

What do you call a cat with eight legs that likes to swim?
An octopuss.

Why did the cat join the Red Cross?
Because she wanted to be a first-aid kit.

Who was the most powerful cat in China?
Chairman Miaow.

What do you get if you cross a cat with a bottle of vinegar?
A sourpuss.

What's cleverer than a talking cat?
A spelling bee.

What do you get if you cross a cat with a canary?
A peeping tom.

How do you know that cats are sensible creatures?
They never cry over spilt milk.

What do you get if you cross a cat with Father
Christmas?
Santa Claws.

How do you put the cat out?
Stand on his tail.

Why did the cat frown when she walked past the hen house?
Because she heard fowl language.

There were three cats in a boat.
One jumped overboard. How many were left?
None. They were all copycats.

What is white, sugary, has whiskers and floats on the sea?
A catameringue.

Why do tomcats fight?
Because they like raising a stink.

Why is a crazy marmalade cat like a biscuit?
They're both ginger nuts.

What do you call a cat that has eaten a whole duck?
A duck-filled-fatty-puss.

What kind of cat should you take into the desert?
A thirst-aid kitty.

Why do cats chase birds?
For a lark.

What do cats read in the mornings?
Mewspapers.

On what should you mount a statue of your cat?
On a caterpillar.

How is a cat stretched over a bed like a coin?
Because he has his head on one side and his tail on
the other.

Which cat purrs more than any other?
A purrsian cat of course.

How do you spell "mousetrap" in three letters?
C-A-T.

What do you get if you cross a Tomcat with a Peking-ese?
A Peking Tom.

Why did the cat put the letter "M" into the fridge?
Because it turns "ice" into "mice."

When the cat's away...
the house smells better.

Why was the cat so small?
It only drank condensed milk.

Why did the cat cross the road?
Because it was the chicken's day off.

What works in the circus, walks a tightrope and has claws?
An acrocat.

What do you call a cat wearing shoes?
Puss in Boots.

What do cats call a bowl full of mice?
A purrfect meal.

What's another way to describe a cat?
A heat-seeking missile.

What did the cat do when he swallowed some
cheese?
He waited by the mousehole with baited breath.

Why are cats longer in the evening than they are in
the morning?
Because they're let out in the evening and taken in
in the morning.

What happened when the cat swallowed a coin?
There was money in the kitty.

Why did the cat sleep under the car?
Because she wanted to wake up oily in the morning.

Well doggone!

If you have a dog, chances are that it's a labrador retriever. That's the most popular kind of dog to have in Britain and the United States. If you have a male dog I bet he's called Sam or if it's a female, is she called Trixie? Those are the two most popular names for dogs. But did you know that an Irish Wolfhound – one of the biggest dogs around – is as tall as a schoolboy and that a dachshund – one of the smallest – is only as high as three apples piled on top of one another. And how do you stop your dog barking in the hall? Put him in the kitchen.

What did the cowboy say when the bear ate Lassie?
"Well, doggone!"

What do you get if you take a really big dog out for a walk?
A Great Dane out.

What kind of meat do you give to a stupid dog?
Chump chops.

What sort of clothes does a pet dog wear?
A petticoat.

What do you get if you cross a sheepdog with a rose?
A collie-flower.

Why did the dachshund bite the woman's ankle?
Because he was short and couldn't reach any higher.

Why did the snowman call his dog Frost?
Because frost bites.

Why did the poor dog chase his own tail?
He was trying to make both ends meet.

Where does a Rottweiller sit in the cinema?
Anywhere he wants to!

What did the angry father sing when he found his
slippers chewed up by the new puppy?
"I must throw that doggie out the window."

What's the difference between dogs and fleas?
Dogs can have fleas but fleas can't have dogs.

Why do dogs wag their tails?
Because no one will wag them for them.

What happened to the dog who ate nothing but garlic?
His bark was much worse than his bite.

Why do dogs bury bones in the ground?
Because you can't bury them in the trees.

What happened when the dog went to the flea circus?
It stole the show.

How can you tell if you have a stupid dog?
It chases parked cars.

What do you get if you cross a dog with Concorde?
A jet setter.

Why did the dog wear white sneakers?
Because his brown boots were at the cobblers.

What do you get if you cross a giraffe with a dog?
An animal that barks at low-flying aircraft.

Where do Eskimos train their dogs?
In the mush room.

What's the difference between Father Christmas and a warm dog?
Father Christmas wears a whole suit, a dog just pants.

When is the most likely time that a stray dog will walk into your house?
When the door is open.

What do you get if you cross a dog with a cheetah?
A dog that chases cars – and catches them!

What happens when it rains cats and dogs?
You can step in a poodle.

What kind of dog does Dracula have?
A bloodhound.

What's the only kind of dog you can eat?
A hot dog.

What kind of dog sounds like you could eat it?
A sausage dog.

What did the starving Dalmation say when he had a meal?
"That hit the spots."

What do you do if your dog swallows your pen?
Use a pencil instead.

Why don't dogs make good dancers?
Because they have two left feet.

What do you get if you cross a Rottweiller with a hyena?
I don't know but if it laughs I'll join in.

What do dogs have that no other animal has?
Puppy dogs.

What do you call an alcoholic dog?
A whino.

What is a dog's favorite sport?
Formula 1 drooling.

What is a dog's favorite food.
Anything that is on your plate.

What dog wears contact lenses?
A cock-eyed spaniel.

What is a dog's favorite flower?
Anything in your garden.

What is a dog's favorite hobby?
Collecting fleas.

How many seasons are there in a dog's life?
Just the one – the moulting season.

Why is it called a "litter" of puppies?
Because they mess up the whole house.

How do you stop a dog smelling?
Put a clothes peg on his nose.

When is the best time to take a Rottweiler for a walk?
Anytime he wants to go.

When does a dog go "moo"?
When it is learning a foreign language.

What kind of dog chases anything red?
A bulldog.

What kind of dog wears a uniform and medals?
A guard dog.

What do you call an Alsation in jeans and a sweater?
A plain clothes police dog.

What do you get if you cross a sheepdog with a jelly?
The collie-wobbles.

Why do you need a license for a dog and not for a cat?
Cats can't drive.

What do you call a dog in the middle of a muddy road?
A mutt in a rut.

When is a black dog not a black dog?
When it's a grayhound.

What do you get if you cross a dog with a blind mole?
A dog that keeps barking up the wrong tree.

What do you get if you cross a gun dog with a phone?
A golden receiver.

What do you get if you cross an Australian dog with a Beatle?
Dingo Starr.

What happens to a dog that keeps eating bits off the table?
He gets splinters in his mouth.

What do you get if you cross a dog with a skunk?
Rid of the dog!

What do you get if you cross a Rottweiller with a computer?
A computer with lots of bites.

What do you get if you cross a dog with a kangaroo?
A dog that has somewhere to put its own lead.

What do you get if you cross a dog with a sheep?
A sheep that can round itself up.

What do you get if you cross a dog with a lion?
A terrified postman.

What do you get if you cross a dog with a frog?
A dog that can lick you from the other side of the road.

What do you get if you cross two young dogs with a pair
of headphones?
Hush puppies.

What do you call a litter of young dogs who have come
in from the snow?
Slush puppies.

What do you call a dog with no legs?
It doesn't matter what you call him, he still won't
come.

How do you feel if you cross a sheepdog with a melon?
Melon-collie.

What do you call a black Eskimo dog?
A dusky husky.

What do you get if you cross a cocker spaniel, a poodle
and a rooster?
Cockerpoodledoo.

What do you call a sheepdog's tail that can tell stories?
A shaggy dog's tale.

Why do dogs run in circles?
It's hard to run in squares.

How did the little Scottish dog feel when he saw a monster?
Terrier-fied.

How do you find your dog if he's lost in the woods?
Just put your ear to a tree and listen for the bark.

Ready,
Teddy, go...

Did you know that the laziest animal in the world is the koala? It sleeps for 22 hours a day! Polar bears are one of the heaviest animals in the world weighing around 1,300 pounds – the weight of ten men! Polar bears have a thin, third eyelid. This helps to protect their eyes from the bright sunlight shining off the snow – a bit like sunglasses! And what does a panda pack when he goes on holiday? Just the bear necessities!

Why was the little bear so spoiled?
Because its mother panda'd to its every whim.

What animal do you look like when you get into the bath?
A little bear.

Why shouldn't you take a bear to the zoo?
Because they'd rather go to the cinema.

What do you call a big white bear with a hole in his middle?
A polo bear.

What should you call a bald teddy?
Fred bear.

Why do polar bears like bald men?
Because they have a great, white, bear place.

What is a bear's favorite drink?
Koka-Koala.

Why is a polar bear cheap to have as a pet?
It lives on ice.

What kind of money do polar bears use?
Ice lolly.

What do you get if you cross a skunk with a bear.
Winnie the Pooh.

Have you ever hunted bear?
No, but I've been shooting in my shorts.

What do polar bears have for lunch?
Ice burger.

What do you get if you cross a teddy bear with a pig?
A teddy boar.

What do Alexander the Great and Winnie the Pooh have in common?
They both have "the" as their middle names.

Why do bears have fur coats?
Because they'd look stupid in anoraks.

What's a teddy bear's favorite pasta?
Tagliateddy.

How do you hire a teddy bear?
Put him on stilts.

How do you start a teddy bear race?
Ready, teddy, go.

Hickory, dickory, dock...

Did you know that hamsters have big pouches in their cheeks that are like shopping bags? They go out and fill up these "bags" with nuts and seeds then scuttle back into their home where they massage their cheeks to get the food out. Sometimes they can collect so much food it weighs as much as an average human being can eat! Rats can live anywhere and eat anything. In London, England, there are four times as many rats as there are human beings! But do you know which is the biggest mouse in the world? The hippopotamouse!

Who has large antlers, a high voice and wears white gloves?
Mickey Moose.

What is small, furry and smells like bacon?
A hamster.

Why do mice need oiling?
Because they squeak.

What is a mouse's favorite record?
"Please cheese me."

What's a mouse's least favorite record?
"What's up Pussycat."

How do you save a drowning mouse?
Use mouse to mouse resuscitation.

What kind of musical instrument do mice play?
A mouse organ.

Is there a mouse in the house?
No, but there's a moose on the loose.

What are crisp, like milk and go "eek, eek, eek" when you eat them?
Mice Krispies.

What have 12 legs, six eyes, three tails and can't see?
Three blind mice.

What do mice do when they're at home?
Mousework.

Where do hamsters come from?
Hamsterdam.

What did Tom get when he locked Jerry in the freezer?
Mice cubes.

When should a mouse carry an umbrella?
When it's raining cats and dogs.

What do you get if you try to cross a mouse with a skunk?
Dirty looks from the mouse.

What squeaks as it solves crimes?
Miami Mice.

Why do mice have long tails?
Well, they'd look silly with long hair.

What is small, furry and brilliant at sword fights?
A mouseketeer.

What do you call a mouse that can pick up an
elephant?
Sir.

What do rodents say when they play bingo?
"Eyes down for a full mouse."

What is small, has a long tail and works with the police?
A gerbil shepherd dog.

What does a twelve-pound mouse say to a cat?
"Here kitty, kitty, kitty."

Oh, for the wings of a bird

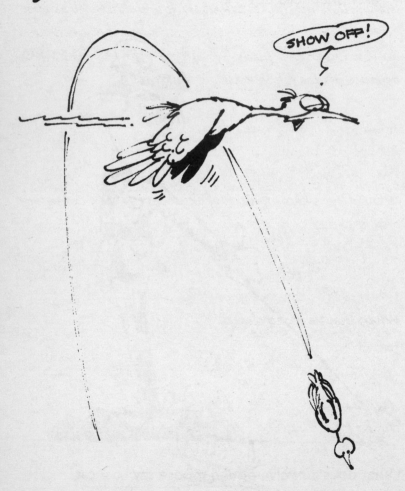

The biggest bird in the world that can fly is the Great Bustard (yes, that's Bustard) which weighs about 45 pounds – the size of a small child. The bird with the longest wingspan in the world is called the Marabou Stork which has a spread of 13 feet. The fastest bird in the world is the Spine-tailed Swift which can fly at over 100 mph, which is faster than some small planes! And do you know why birds fly south in the winter? Well, because it's too far to walk, of course.

What kind of bird opens doors?
A kiwi.

What do you call a bunch of chickens playing hide-and-seek?
Fowl play.

When is the best time to buy budgies?
When they're going cheap.

How do you get a parrot to talk properly?
Send him to polytechnic.

What is a duck's favorite TV show?
The feather forecast.

Which birds steal soap from the bath?
Robber ducks.

What birds spend all their time on their knees?
Birds of prey.

What do baby swans dance to?
Cygnet-ure tunes.

Where do birds meet for coffee?
In a nest-cafe.

Why is a sofa like a roast chicken?
Because they're both full of stuffing.

What do you get if your budgie flies into the blender?
Shredded Tweet.

What did they call the canary that flew into the pastry dish?
Tweetie Pie.

What is a polygon?
A dead parrot.

How do you get a cut-price parrot?
Plant bird seed.

Which bird is always out of breath?
A puffin.

What is a parrot's favorite game?
Hide and Speak.

What flies through the jungle singing opera?
The parrots of Penzance.

What kind of birds do you usually find locked up?
Jail-birds.

What's got six legs and can fly long distances?
Three swallows.

What do you get if you cross a woodpecker with a carrier pigeon?
A bird who knocks before delivering its message.

What happened when the owl lost his voice?
He didn't give a hoot.

Why did the parrot wear a raincoat?
Because she wanted to be Polly unsaturated.

What do you get if you cross a duck with a firework?
A firequacker.

What do you call a crate of ducks?
A box of quackers.

Where do blind sparrows go for treatment?
The Birds Eye counter.

How does a bird with a broken wing manage to land safely?
With its sparrowchute.

What do owls sing when it is raining?
"Too wet to woo."

What do you call a bird that lives underground?
A mynah bird.

What do you call a woodpecker with no beak?
A headbanger.

What do you get if you cross a parrot with a centipede?
A great walkie-talkie.

What language do birds speak?
Pigeon English.

What do you get if you cross a parrot with a wood-pecker?
A bird that talks in morse code.

What do you get if you cross a parrot with a shark?
A bird that will talk your ear off.

Why did the owl 'owl?
Because the woodpecker would peck 'er.

What do you call a very rude bird?
A mockingbird.

What's another name for a clever duck?
A wise quacker.

What do parrots eat?
Polyfilla.

Where do birds invest their money?
In the stork market.

What bird tastes just like butter?
A stork.

What did the gamekeeper say to the lord of the manor?
"The pheasants are revolting."

What is green and pecks on trees?
Woody Wood Pickle.

How do you know that owls are cleverer than chickens?
Have you ever heard of Kentucky-fried owl?

What is the definition of a robin?
A bird who steals.

What happens when ducks fly upside down?
They quack up.

What do you give a sick bird?
Tweetment.

What do you call a Scottish parrot?
A Macaw.

Old Macdonald had a farm

Did you know that there are 12,664 *million* chickens in the world? Think of that when you bite into your next chicken nugget. In some countries there are far more sheep than humans – like the Falkland Islands with 338 sheep per person! There are some countries where there are very few pigs because the people there are not allowed to eat pork, but China has more pigs than any other country with nearly 425 million. The United States has more cows than any other country, and do you know which state is the cows' favorite? Moo York!

Where do milkshakes come from?
Excited cows.

Why did the foal cough?
Because he was a little horse.

What's the best way to make a bull sweat?
Put him in a tight jumper.

What do you get if you cross a chicken with a bell?
A bird that has to wring its own neck.

Why did the bull rush?
Because it saw the cow slip.

What animal always goes to bed with its shoes on?
A horse.

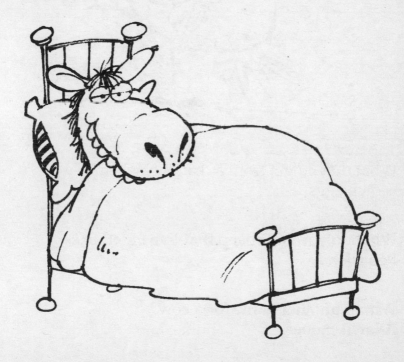

What do you call a sheep with no legs or head?
A cloud.

What do you get from a drunk chicken?
Scotch eggs.

What do you call sheep that live together?
Pen friends.

What's another name for a cow?
A lawn-mooer.

What do you call a pig thief?
A hamburglar.

Why does a rooster watch TV?
For hentertainment.

What do you give a pony with a cold?
Cough Stirrup.

What do you get if you cross a hen with a dog?
Pooched eggs.

What do you call a crate of ducks?
A box of quackers.

What do you get if a sheep walks under a cloud?
A sheep that's under the weather.

What do you call a chicken in a shellsuit?
An egg.

What kind of tie does a pig wear?
Pig's tie.

What do you get if you cross a sheep with a kangaroo?
A woolly jumper.

What did the baby chick say when he saw his
mother sitting on an orange?
"Dad, dad, look what marma-laid!"

What game do cows play at parties?
Moosical chairs.

What has four legs and flies?
A pig.

What kind of things does a farmer talk about
when he is milking cows?
Udder nonsense.

Why did the chicken cross the road at the
fairground?
To get to the other ride.

Why did the pig go to the casino?
To play the slop machine.

What happens when geese land in a volcano?
They cook their own gooses.

What do you get from an Alaskan cow?
Cold cream.

What do you get if you cross pigs with a lot of grapes?
A swine glut.

Why did the starstruck chicken cross the road?
To see Gregory Peck.

Why did the Roman chicken cross the road?
Because she was afraid someone would Caesar.

Why did the dirty chicken cross the road?
For some fowl purpose.

What is a pig's favorite ballet?
Swine Lake.

What do you get if you feed gunpowder to a
chicken?
An egg-splosion.

Why did the baby turkey bolt down his food?
Because he was a little gobbler.

What did the farmer call the cow that wouldn't
give him any milk?
An udder failure.

What do you get if you cross a chicken with a
cement mixer?
A brick-layer.

How do sheep keep warm in winter?
Central bleating.

What do you call an arctic cow?
An eskimoo.

What do you call a pig with no clothes on?
Streaky bacon.

What do you call a pig that took a plane?
Swine flu.

What's the easiest way to count a herd of cattle?
Use a cowculator.

What kind of bird lays electric eggs?
A battery hen.

What did the lovesick bull say to the cow?
"When I fall in love it will be for heifer."

What do you get if you cross a cow with a
camel?
Lumpy milkshakes.

What do you call a sleeping bull?
A bulldozer.

What do you get if you cross a steer with a
tadpole?
A bullfrog.

How do you stop a rooster crowing on Sunday?
Eat him on Saturday.

If you had fifteen cows and five goats what would you have?
Plenty of milk.

What do you call a pig who's been arrested for dangerous driving?
A road hog.

What do you get if you sit under a cow?
A pat on the head.

Why was the farmer hopping mad?
Because someone had trodden on his corn.

Why do ducks have webbed feet?
To stamp out forest fires.

How do chickens dance?
Chick to chick.

Why did the ram fall over the cliff?
He didn't see the ewe turn.

What do you get if you cross a cow with an
octopus?
A cow that can milk itself.

When do ducks get up?
At the quack of dawn.

Who takes the shortest time to prepare for a
holiday – a rooster or an elephant?
The rooster because he only has to take his comb
whereas an elephant must take a trunk.

What's another way to describe a duck?
A chicken with snowshoes.

What do they call a "quack"?
A doctor who ducks the law.

What smells worse than a pig in a sty?
Two pigs in a sty.

Why did the rooster refuse to fight?
Because he was chicken.

Why don't lambs like arithmetic?
Because when they add five and three they get
ate.

What do you get if you feed a cow money?
Rich milk.

What's the definition of a goose?
An animal that grows down as it grows up.

What's a cow's favorite vegetable?
A cowat.

How do you take a pig to hospital?
By hambulance.

What do you call a bull who tells jokes?
Laugh-a-bull.

Why is it called a "herd" of cattle?
Well, have you "herd" the sound they make?

Why were the hens lying on their backs with
their legs in the air?
Because eggs were going up.

What do cows like to dance to?
Any kind of moosic you like.

Why did the unwashed chicken cross the road
twice?
Because he was a dirty double crosser.

Who tells chicken jokes?
Comedihens.

What is the opposite of cock-a-doodle-doo?
Cock-a-doodle-don't.

What do you call a crazy chicken?
A cuckoo-cluck.

What do you call a joke book for chickens?
A yolk book.

What's the best way to keep milk from turning
sour?
Leave it inside the cow.

What do you get if you cross a pile of mud with a pig?
A groundhog.

How do you fit more pigs on your farm?
Build a sty-scraper.

What do you call the story of The Three Little Pigs?
A pigtail.

What do you get if you cross a cow, a sheep and a goat?
The milky baa kid.

What do you give a sick pig?
Oinkment.

Which bull led 3,000 elephants over the Alps and conquered Italy?
Hanni-bull.

What do you say if you see a flying pig?
"I see bacon's going up."

What kind of doctor treats ducks?
A quack.

What is a cow's favorite TV show?
Dr Moo.

Why was the lamb told off for being rude?
He wouldn't say "thank ewe" to his mum.

What is a duck's favorite dance?
The quackstep.

Which dance will a chicken not do?
The foxtrot.

What did the well-mannered sheep say to his
friend at the field gate?
After ewe.

Where do cows go on a Saturday night?
To the moo-vies.

Why did the farmer call his pig "Ink"?
Because he kept running out of the pen.

How do you hire a horse?
Buy it two pairs of stilts.

What do they call a chicken inspector?
A cluck watcher.

What's white, lives in the Himalayas and lays eggs?
The Abominable Snow Chicken.

What goes oom, oom?
A cow walking backwards.

What gives milk, says "Moo, moo" and makes all your dreams come true?
Your dairy godmother.

Why did the cow go over the hill?
Because it couldn't go under it.

How do hens know how to lay eggs?
They take eggsaminations.

What did the duck say when she bought some lipstick?
Put it on the bill.

What made the cow jump over the moon?
The milkmaid had cold hands.

Why didn't the little horse get a bicycle for his birthday?
Each time he asked, his mother said "Neigh!"

Where do you take sick ponies?
To the horsepital.

Why did Bo Peep lose her sheep?
She had a crook with her.

Where do sheep get shorn?
At the baa baas.

What goes "peck, bang, peck, bang, peck, bang"?
A bunch of chickens in a field full of balloons.

What is a horse's favorite sport?
Stable tennis.

What is the slowest racehorse in the world?
A clotheshorse.

Why do pigs never recover from illness?
Because you have to kill them before you cure
them.

Where does a woodsman keep his pigs?
In a hog cabin.

Why do cows like being told jokes?
Because they like being amoosed.

What would happen if bulls could fly?
You would have to carry an umbrella all the time
and beef would go up.

Tiger, tiger, burning bright

Have you ever been cheated by a cheetah, or tied-up by a tiger, lied to by a lion or run over by a jaguar? No? Well, did you know that a cheetah is so powerful that it can accelerate faster than a sports car – so don't ever bother to race one! Also, tigers can leap enormous distances – they could even reach the top of a bus in one jump. Tigers are bigger than lions, even though a big male lion can weigh as much as two men. And a leopard? Well, a leopard is just an animal that is easy to spot (geddit? easy to *spot*! Oh well...)

How are tigers like sergeants in the army?
They both wear stripes.

What is a lion's favorite food?
Baked beings.

What do you get if you cross a tiger with a sheep?
A stripey sweater.

What do you get if you cross a tiger with a kangaroo?
A stripey jumper.

What do you get if you cross a tiger with a snowman?
Frostbite.

What do tigers wear in bed?
Stripey pyjamas.

How does a leopard change its spots?
When it gets tired of one spot it just moves to another.

What happened to the leopard who took a bath three times a day?
After a week he was spotless.

If a four-legged animal is a quadruped and a two-legged animal is a biped, what's a tiger?
A stri-ped.

What do you call a show full of lions?
The mane event.

What was the name of the film about a killer lion
that swam underwater?
"Claws."

What does the lion say to his friends before they go
out hunting for food?
"Let us prey."

What did the lion say to his cubs when he taught
them to hunt?
"Don't go over the road till you see the zebra
crossing."

Why do you never see zebras or antelopes at
Victoria Station?
Because it's a "mane-lion" station.

What do the big cats have for breakfast in Africa?
Cheetabix.

What do you call a trainer who sticks his hand in a
lion's mouth?
Lefty.

Did you hear about the lion's show?
It was a roaring success.

"Tiger, tiger, burning bright,
Someone's set your tail alight!"

What do you get if you cross a leopard with a tiger?
A terrible fashion mistake.

What's striped and goes round and round?
A tiger in a revolving door.

On which side does a tiger have most of his stripes?
On the outside.

Why did the tiger paint out his black stripes?
So that he could hide in a jar of marmalade.

What's the silliest name you can give a tiger?
Spot.

Why don't leopards escape from the zoo for long?
Because they're easily spotted.

What's the difference between a tiger and a lion?
A tiger has the mane part missing.

What flies around your light at night and can bite off
your head?
A tiger moth.

What happened when the lion ate the comedian?
He felt funny.

What do you call a lion who has eaten your mother's
sister?
An aunt-eater.

What do you get if you cross a leopard with a
watchdog?
A terrified postman.

What is the fiercest flower in the garden?
The tiger lily.

What does a lion brush his mane with?
A catacomb.

Why did the lion feel sick after he'd eaten the priest?
Because it's hard to keep a good man down.

On which day do lions eat people?
Chewsday.

What is the most breathless thing on television?
The Pink Panter Show.

When is a lion not a lion?
When he turns into his cage.

Why is the desert lion everyone's favorite at
Christmas?
Because he has sandy claws.

How does a lion greet the other animals in the field?
"Pleased to eat you!"

What happens when a lion runs into an express train
at the station?
It's the end of the lion.

What do you call a lion wearing a cravat and a flower
in its mane?
A dandy lion.

Why was the lion-tamer fined?
He parked on a yellow lion.

Which big cat should you never play cards with?
A cheetah.

What's striped and bouncy?
A tiger on a pogo stick.

What do tigers sing at Christmas?
"Jungle bells, jungle bells..."

What happened to the man who tried to cross a lion
with a goat?
He had to get a new goat.

What did the lioness say to the cub chasing a hunter?
"Stop playing with your food."

How can you get a set of teeth put in for free?
Smack a lion.

Beautiful, briney sea

How many types of fish have you seen? Well there are at least 20,000 different types of fish in the sea and rivers around the world. In fact there could be up to 20,000 more in some of the really, really, really deep parts of the sea that no one has been in yet. The world's largest fish is the whale shark which is more than 50 feet long and weighs several tons. The smallest fish is the tiny goby which is less than half an inch long and lives in fresh water in the Philippines. But hey, do you know which is the most famous fish in the sea? Well the starfish, of course!

What game do fish like playing the most?
Name that tuna.

What happens when sharks take their clothes off?
They go sharkers.

What do naked fish play with?
Bare-a-cudas

What do you call a dangerous fish who drinks too much?
A beer-a-cuda.

Which fish can perform operations?
A sturgeon.

What do you get if you cross a big fish with an electricity pylon?
An electric shark.

Why is a fish easy to weigh?
Because it has its own scales.

Who has eight guns and terrorizes the ocean?
Billy the Squid.

What is a dolphin's favorite TV show?
Whale of Fortune.

Where does seaweed look for a job?
In the "kelp-wanted" ads.

What fish goes up the river at 100mph?
A motor pike.

Why are fish boots the warmest ones to wear?
Because they have electric 'eels.

What did the boy fish say to his girlfriend?
"Your plaice or mine?"

How could the dolphin afford to buy a house?
He prawned everything.

Why are dolphins cleverer than humans?
Within three hours they can train a man to stand at
the side of a pool and feed them fish.

Where do little fishes go every morning?
To plaice school.

What kind of fish will help you hear better?
A herring aid.

What kind of money do fishermen make?
Net profits.

What do you call a fish with no eyes?
Fsh.

What happened to the cold jellyfish?
It set.

To whom do fish go to borrow money?
The loan shark.

Why are goldfish orange?
The water makes them rusty.

Who held the baby octopus to ransom?
Squidnappers.

Why did the whale cross the road?
To get to the other tide.

What is a whale's favorite game?
Swallow the leader.

Why are sardines the stupidest fish in the sea?
Because they climb into tins, close the lid and leave the key outside.

What was the Tsar of Russia's favorite fish?
Tsardines.

Who sleeps at the bottom of the sea?
Jack the Kipper.

What do you get if you cross an abbot with a trout?
Monkfish.

What bit of fish doesn't make sense?
The piece of cod that passeth all understanding.

How do fish go into business?
They start on a small scale.

What do you get if you cross a trout with an
apartment?
A flat fish.

What do you get if you cross a salmon, a bird's leg and
a hand?
Birdsthigh fish fingers.

What did the boy octopus say to the girl octopus?
I wanna hold your hand, hand, hand, hand, hand,
hand, hand, hand.

What do you call a big fish who makes you an offer you
can't refuse?
The Codfather.

How does an octopus go to war?
Well-armed.

What is dry on the outside, filled with water and
blows up buildings?
A fish tank.

What do fish sing to each other?
Salmon-chanted Evening.

Where do shellfish go to borrow money?
To the prawn-broker.

What fish do road-menders use?
Pneumatic krill.

What's the coldest fish in the sea?
A blue whale.

Where are most fish found?
Between the head and the tail.

What lives in the ocean, is grouchy and hates
neighbors?
A hermit crab.

Where do you find a down-and-out octopus?
On squid row.

What did the sardine call the submarine?
A can of people.

What's the difference between a fish and a piano?
You can't tuna fish.

What kind of horse can swim underwater without coming up for air?
A seahorse.

What kind of noise annoys an oyster?
A noisy noise annoys an oyster. (Try saying that fast!)

Where do you weigh whales?
At a whale weigh station.

What do you get from a bad-tempered shark?
As far away as possible.

What kind of fish goes well with ice-cream?
Jellyfish.

What is the best way to communicate with a fish?
Drop it a line.

Which part of a fish weighs the most?
It's scales.

Why did the lobster blush?
Because the sea weed.

What kind of fish is useful in freezing weather?
Skate.

What happened to the shark who swallowed a bunch
of keys?
He got lockjaw.

What fish only swims at night?
A starfish.

How do the little fish get to school?
By octobus.

1st kipper: "Smoking's bad for you."
2nd kipper: "It's OK, I've been cured."

Which fish go to heaven when they die?
Angel fish.

Where do fish wash?
In a river basin.

What, Why, Where?

How do you know if your best friend is a real animal? If he attracts fleas. What's the definition of a zoo? Somewhere where your mum and dad have to pay for you all to go in and then have to pay again to get your beastly little brother out again. How many of the animals in this next set of jokes have you seen at the zoo already? Make a note of the ones you haven't seen and check them off next time you go there.

What's the difference between a milkmaid and a seagull?
One skims milk and the other skims water.

What's black and white and red all over?
A sunburnt penguin.

What is the proper name for the water otter?
A kettle.

What is Florence the Penguin's nickname?
Ice-Flo.

Where do tadpoles turn into frogs?
In the croakroom.

What does a tortoise do on the road?
About one mile per day.

Why are wolves like playing cards?
Because they both come in packs.

What do you get if you cross a skunk with a
boomerang?
A nasty smell that keeps coming back.

Why did the antelope?
Nobody Gnu.

What's the definition of a giraffe?
The highest form of animal life.

Why did the porcupine wear spikes to the party?
Because he was a sharp dresser.

What kind of animals use nutcrackers?
Toothless squirrels.

What do toads sit on?
Toadstools.

What do you get if you cross a porcupine with a giraffe?
A giant toothbrush.

What is a frog's favorite drink?
Croak-a-cola.

What do you get if you cross a hyena with a
water butt?
A barrel of laughs.

What happens to illegally-parked frogs?
They get toad away.

What do you say if you meet a toad?
Wart's new?

What's hairy, rules England and loves bananas?
King Henry the Ape.

What do you get when you cross a stallion with a possum?
A horse that hangs by its tail.

What's the difference between a stupid person and a gorilla?
The gorilla peels the banana before he eats it.

What weighs three tons, is gray and flies?
A hippo on a hang glider.

What does a frog order in a fast-food restaurant?
A burger and flies.

What is the biggest laundry problem giraffes have?
Ring around the collar.

What do you get if you pour hot water down a rabbit hole?
Hot cross bunnies.

What is a squirrel's favorite ballet?
The nutcracker.

Which is the stupidest monkey in the jungle?
The chumpanzee.

Why did the lizard go on a diet?
It weighed too much for its scales.

Why were animals pleased when the gnus left the jungle?
Because no gnus is good gnus.

What would you wear if you had a smelly donkey?
An ass mask.

What do you get if you cross a grizzly bear with vanishing cream?
No one knows because it's gone before you can see it.

What does an angry kangaroo do?
It gets hopping mad.

Where do you find hippos?
It depends where you left them.

How do you tell the difference between a hippo and a banana?
Try eating a hippo.

When do kangaroos celebrate their birthdays?
In a leap year.

What pet makes the loudest noise?
A trum-pet.

What pet always sticks close?
A limpet.

How do you catch a squirrel?
Crouch down and make a noise like an acorn.

What's white outside, green inside and hops?
A frog sandwich.

What do you get if you give a monkey sugar and egg-white?
A meringue-utang.

What's green and can jump a mile a minute?
A frog with hiccoughs.

What's scaly, has a hard shell and bounces?
A tortoise on a pogo stick.

Why is a psychiatrist like a squirrel?
Because they're both surrounded by nuts.

How did the rabbit get to Australia?
He flew by hareplane.

What is black and white and very noisy?
A zebra with a drum kit.

What did one deer say to another deer?
"Man, I wish I had your doe."

What is a crocodile's favorite game?
Snap.

What did the croaking frog say to his friend?
"I think I've got a person in my throat."

What animal is it best to be on a cold day?
A little otter.

How is a skunk different from a rabbit?
A skunk uses a cheaper deodorant.

What's worse than a giraffe with a sore throat?
A centipede with chilblains.

What did the bus conductor say to the frog?
Hop on.

What do gnus read in the morning?
The gnus paper.

What's got two humps and changes color?
A camel-ion.

What do rabbits call mobile homes?
Wheel-burrows.

What do you call an animal that's half parrot and half tiger?
Anything it lets you call it.

Which American president had very sharp teeth?
Jaws Washington.

Why do seals lie on rocks?
Because if they lay under them they'd get squashed.

What do reindeer say before they tell a joke?
"This one will sleigh you!"

What do you do if you step on a gorilla's foot?
Say sorry, of course.

What's full of animals and quite a relief?
A zoo-loo.

What's brown on the inside, brown on the
outside and jumps a lot?
A kangaroo on rye.

What is out of bounds?
An exhausted kangaroo.

What did the donkey say when he saw he only
had thistles to eat?
"Thistle have to do."

What did the dog say to the flea?
"Don't bug me."

What goes "croak, croak" in the fog?
A frog horn.

What's green, dangerous and good at adding up?
A young crocodile with a calculator.

How can you tell a rabbit from a gorilla?
Just try getting a gorilla into a rabbit hutch.

What's a "twip"?
It's what a wabbit makes when he wides a twain.

How do you catch a monkey?
Hang upside down and make a noise like a
banana.

What animal with two humps can be found at
the North Pole?
A lost camel.

What do you call a sick crocodile?
An illigator.

What's black and white, smelly and has 16
wheels?
A skunk on roller skates.

Why does a chimpanzee scratch himself?
Because he's the only one who knows where it
itches.

What do you get if you cross an elk with a
chocolate bar?
Chocolate mousse.

What did the beaver say to the tree?
It's been nice gnawing you.

What is a porcupine's favorite food?
Prickled onions.

Why do buffalo always travel in herds?
Because they are afraid of getting mugged by
elephants.

What is the cheapest animal in the zoo to feed?
A giraffe because a little goes a long way.

What to you call a laughing hippo?
A happypotamus.

Where do you take a frog with bad eyesight?
To the hoptician.

What has a big lumpy body, 20 hairy legs and
blue slimey feet?
I don't know, but it's crawling up your leg.

What's another great way to catch a squirrel?
Climb up a tree and act like a nut.

What did the short-sighted porcupine say to the
cactus?
Is that you mama?

Why do flamingoes stand on one leg?
Because if they lifted it up they'd fall over.

What is yellow and very dangerous?
Shark-infested custard.

What do you call a camel with three humps?
Humphrey.

What do gorillas use to mend their cars?
A monkey wrench.

What do you call a happy kangaroo?
A hop-timist.

What did one flea say to another after a night out?
"Shall we walk home or take a dog?"

Where do lions go if they lose their tails?
The retailers.

What's the difference between a buffalo and a bison?
You can't wash your hands in a buffalo.

What do you call a penguin in the desert?
Lost.

What do you get if you cross a giraffe with a rooster?
An animal that can wake you up on the top floor.

What do you get if you cross a turkey with an octopus?
A leg for everyone at Christmas.

Why couldn't the butterfly go to the dance?
Because it was a moth-ball.

What goes buzz-choo, buzz-choo?
A bee with a cold.

What's green and yellow and goes in a roll with onions?
A hot frog.

Why are frogs happier than cats?
Because frogs croak all the time and cats only croak nine times.

What happens if you cross a gorilla and a skunk?
It always get a seat on the bus.

Who ate his animals two by two?
Noah Shark.

What do you call a deer with one eye?
No idea.

What do you call a deer with one eye and no legs?
Still, no idea.

Why do giraffes have such long necks?
Because their feet smell so bad.

Why was the sick boy about to croak?
Because he swallowed a frog.

What is black and white, black and white, black
and white?
A penguin rolling down a hill.

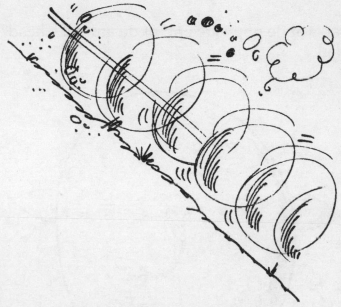

What's very tall, yellow and pretty?
A giraffe-adil.

What is a slug?
A snail with a housing problem.

Which brand of petrol do snails prefer?
Shell.

What do you get if you cross a hyena with a parrot?
A creature that laughs at its own jokes.

Why are gorillas big and hairy?
So you can tell them apart from gooseberries.

What is at de opposite end of de animal's head?
De tail.

Where does a huge rhinoceros sleep?
Anywhere it wants to.

Which monkeys are white and fluffy?
Meringue-utangs.

What do you get if you cross a skunk with an astronaut?
An animal that stinks to high heaven.

Why are kangaroos looking forward to the millennium?
Because it's a leap-year.

What's the difference between a monkey and a politician?
You can hold a sensible conversation with a monkey.

What is the wettest kind of animal?
A raindeer.

How do you get a wild duck?
Buy a tame one and annoy it.

What is a horse's favorite game?
Stable tennis.

What do you call a kangaroo cowboy?
Hopalong Cassidy.

What do you get if you cross a kangaroo with a
ferry boat?
A hoppercraft.

What do you call animals that fall from the sky?
Raindeer.

How do you stop a mole digging in your
garden?
Hide his spade.

What is the definition of a zebra?
A horse wearing venetian blinds.

What is red, freezing and dangerous?
Shark-infested strawberry ice cream.

What animals eat petrol?
Otter-mobiles.

What did the skunk say when the wind changed?
"Now it all comes back to me."

Which is the most dangerous animal in the Northern Hemisphere?
Yak the Ripper.

What do you get if you cross a hyena with a porcupine?
A hyena that doesn't laugh – it just needles you.

What kind of fur do you get from lions?
As fur away as you can.

What is big, hairy and can fly faster than the speed of sound?
King Koncord.

What is the most talkative animal in the world?
The yak.

What is the definition of a zoo?
A place where humans can visit and animals are barred.

Doctor! Doctor!

Doctor! Doctor! I keep thinking I'm a goat.
How long have you felt this?
Since I was a kid.

Fish: Doctor! Doctor! I can't hear anything.
Doctor: Get a herring aid.

Doctor! Doctor! I think I'm a donkey.
You're taking me for a ride.

Doctor! Doctor! I think I'm a chicken.
Lay on the couch would you?

Doctor! Doctor! I keep thinking I'm a dog.
Lie down on the couch.
I can't, I'm not allowed on the furniture.

Doctor! Doctor! I think I'm a frog.
You're clearly playing too much croquet.

Doctor! Doctor! I think my son's turning into a mouse.
Why do you think that?
Because I've just found him playing Hide and Squeak.

Doctor! Doctor! I think I'm a fly.
Will you come down off the ceiling please.

Doctor! Doctor! I keep thinking I'm a dog out in the cold.
Oh, stop whining.

Doctor! Doctor! My wife thinks she's a bird.
Why couldn't she come here herself?
She doesn't like to come out of her cage.

Doctor! Doctor! I keep seeing green tigers before my eyes.
Have you seen a psychiatrist?
No, only green tigers.

Doctor! Doctor! I think I'm a chicken.
I'd better put you into hospital for a few days.
You can't do that, my family need the eggs.

Doctor! Doctor! I keep seeing frogs before my eyes.
Don't worry, it's just a hoptical illusion.

Doctor! Doctor! I feel as sick as a dog.
Hang on, I'll call the vet.

Doctor! Doctor! I keep thinking everyone I meet is a bird.
Tweet, tweet, tweet, tweet.

Doctor! Doctor! I think my pet vulture's dying of flu.
Vultures don't die of flu.
This one will, it flew under a bus.

Doctor! Doctor! I keep thinking I'm a badger on the road.
Yes, you look a bit run down.

Doctor! Doctor! I think I'm a bumble bee.
Oh, buzz off.

Doctor! Doctor! I'm as insignificant as a mouse. No one takes any notice of me.
Next!

Doctor! Doctor! I've just swallowed a sheep.
How do you feel?
Very baa-aad.

Doctor! Doctor! I keep thinking I'm a cow.
You silly moo.

Doctor! Doctor! I keep thinking I'm a racehorse.
How much do you want to bet that you're not?

Doctor! Doctor! My husband thinks he's a cat. Every
night there's this horrible howling outside my
window.
How do you know it isn't a cat?
No cat would use language like that.

Doctor! Doctor! I keep thinking I'm a duck.
So why have you come to me?
I thought you'd give me a small bill.

Doctor! Doctor! People keep mistaking me for a dog.
Well, I must say your nose is a little dry.

Doctor! Doctor! I keep thinking I'm an elephant.
Well just remember that you're not.
Thanks doctor, I'll never forget.

Doctor! Doctor! My wife thinks she's a goose.
Why hasn't she come here herself?
She can't, she's flown south for the winter.

Doctor! Doctor! I keep thinking I'm a parrot.
Why do you think that?
Why do you think that?
Stop copying me.
Stop copying me. *(You can carry on as long as you like
with this one!)*

Doctor! Doctor! I keep thinking I'm a frog.
All right, hop on the couch.

Doctor! Doctor! I did what you said and ate carrots
like a rabbit to help my eyesight.
Yes, and has it helped?
Well my eyes are getting better but I keep tripping
over my ears.

Waiter! Waiter!

Waiter! Waiter! This chicken's only got one leg.
Perhaps it's been in a fight, sir.
In that case, bring me the winner.

Waiter! Waiter! What kind of bird is this?
Wood pigeon, sir.
Just as I thought – bring me a saw, will you?

Waiter! Waiter! I can't eat this chicken. Call the manager.
It's no good sir, he won't eat it either.

Waiter! Waiter! There's no chicken in the chicken soup. Well there's no horse in the horseradish either, sir.

Waiter! Waiter! There's a fly in my soup.
Don't worry! The frog will surface any minute.

Waiter! Waiter! There's a frog in my soup.
Yes sir, the fly is on holiday.

Waiter! Waiter! Do you have chicken legs?
No, I always walk like this.

Waiter! Waiter! Do you serve lobster?
Bring it in, sir. We're not fussy who we serve here.

Waiter! Waiter! Do you have frog's legs?
No sir, it's just the way I'm standing.

Waiter! Waiter! This fish is very rude.
Yes sir, it doesn't know its plaice.

Waiter! Waiter! There's a frog on my plate.
Sorry sir. It was toad in the hole you ordered wasn't it?

Watier, waiter! This chicken's disgusting.
Yes sir, you asked for grilled foul didn't you?

Waiter! Waiter! There's a crocodile in my soup.
Yes sir, you ordered soup and told me to make it
snappy.

Waiter! Waiter! This fish tastes of dog meat.
Yes sir, it's a Rover sole.

Waiter! Waiter! This tea's not fit for a pig.
Sorry sir, I'll get you something that is.

Names

What do you call a girl with a frog on her head?
Lily.

What do you call a boy with a rabbit on his head?
Warren.

What do you call a boy with a seagull on his head?
Cliff.

What do you call a girl who can make animals better?
Yvette.

What do you call a girl covered in starfish and pebbles?
Sandy.

What do you call a girl with a hard, shiny back?
Michelle.

What do you call a seagull on a choppy sea?
Bob.

What do you call a girl who buzzes all the time?
Bea.

What do you call a boy with a red chest?
Robin.

What do you call a boy with a woodpecker on his back?
Woody.

What do you call a boy who keeps standing on electricity cables?
Flash.

What do you call a Reindeer wearing a number plate?
Reg.

Knock Knock!

Knock Knock!
Who's there?
Turkey.
Turkey who?
Turkey to the right then it'll open.

Knock Knock!
Who's there?
Seagull.
Seagull who?
Seagull over there?
She wants to see you.

Knock Knock!
Who's there?
Puffin.
Puffin who?
Puffin and panting – I've run all the way here.

Knock Knock!
Who's there?
Rat.
Rat who?
Rat-a-tat-tat.

Knock Knock!
Who's there?
Tilly.
Tilly who?
Tilly cows come home.

Knock Knock!
Who's there?
Mouse.
Mouse who?
Mouse-warming present for you.

Knock Knock!
Who's there?
Budgie.
Budgie who?
Budgie up! I want to get in.

Knock Knock!
Who's there?
Bison.
Bison who?
Bison new handles – these ones don't work.

Knock Knock!
Who's there?
Giraffe.
Giraffe who?
Giraffe anything to eat? I'm starving.

Knock Knock!
Who's there?
Janet.
Janet who?
Janet a big fish?

Knock Knock!
Who's there?
Yak.
Yak who?
Yakuse you of preventing me from coming in.

Knock Knock!
Who's there?
Emu.
Emu who?
Emu mother. Let me in!

Knock Knock!
Who's there?
Llama.
Llama who?
Llama's gone off – you must have been burgled.

Knock Knock!
Who's there?
Gnu.
Gnu who?
Don't cry, it can't be that bad.

Knock Knock!
Who's there?
Nell.
Nell who?
Nelly the elephant.

Knock Knock!
Who's there?
Zebra.
Zebra who?
Zebra won't do up. Can you help me?

Knock Knock!
Who's there?
Antelope.
Antelope who?
Antelope and uncle lope of course.

Knock Knock!
Who's there?
Warthog.
Warthog who?
Warthog please – I'm so thirsty.

Knock Knock!
Who's there?
Ape.
Ape who?
Apen the door will you?

Knock Knock!
Who's there?
Ali.
Ali who?
Ali cat.

Knock Knock!
Who's there?
Monkey.
Monkey who?
Monkey won't fit the lock.

Knock Knock!
Who's there?
Chimp.
Chimp who?
Chimp up to the window and take a look.

Knock Knock!
Who's there?
Gorilla.
Gorilla who?
Gorilla some cheese on toast please.

Knock Knock!
Who's there?
Rhino.
Rhino who?
Rhino who you are. Why don't you recognize me?

Knock Knock!
Who's there?
Tristan.
Tristan who?
Tristan elephant not to forget.

Knock Knock!
Who's there?
Hippo.
Hippo who?
Hippo birthday to you, hippo birthday to you.

Knock Knock!
Who's there?
Alligator.
Alligator who.
Alligator shut so I climbed over the wall.

Knock Knock!
Who's there?
Stork.
Stork who?
Stork some deer with me – it's fun.

Knock Knock!
Who's there?
Tarzan.
Tarzan who?
Tarzan moon are in your eyes.

Knock Knock!
Who's there?
Ray.
Ray who?
Rayning cats and dogs.

Knock Knock!
Who's there?
Weevil.
Weevil who?
Weevil make you talk

Knock Knock!
Who's there?
Puma
Puma who?
Puma feet smell! Let me in to wash them.

Knock Knock!
Who's there?
Catsup.
Catsup who?
Catsup a tree and won't come down!

Knock Knock!
Who's there?
Cheetah.
Cheetah who?
Cheetah out of all her money.

Knock Knock!
Who's there?
Ivan.
Ivan who?
Ivan enormous snake in my pocket.

Knock Knock!
Who's there?
Tiger.
Tiger who?
Tiger a look at my new ball.

Knock Knock!
Who's there?
Lioness.
Lioness who?
Lioness new couch I've bought.

Knock Knock!
Who's there?
Panther.
Panther who?
Panther falling down, I need to come inthide.

Knock Knock!
Who's there?
Leopard.
Leopard who?
Leopardle was so deep I got my clothes wet.

Knock Knock!
Who's there?
Parrot.
Parrot who?
Parrotly you live here.

Knock Knock!
Who's there?
Dog.
Dog who?
Doggedly standing at your door.

Knock Knock!
Who's there?
Cat.
Cat who?
Cat you get to the door any faster?

Knock Knock!
Who's there?
Siamese.
Siamese who?
Siamesily pleased, I would like to see you.

Knock Knock!
Who's there?
Cat.
Cat who?
Cat you understand?

Knock Knock!
Who's there?
Moth.
Moth who?
Motht get mythelf a key.

Knock Knock!
Who's there?
Cow.
Cow who?
Cow long do I have to wait out here?

Knock Knock!
Who's there?
Horse.
Horse who?
Horse you know who I am – open up.

Knock Knock!
Who's there?
Pig.
Pig who?
Piggy in the middle.

Knock Knock!
Who's there?
Goose.
Goose who?
Gooses a kiss.

Knock Knock!
Who's there?
Bug.
Bug who?
Bug Rogers.

Knock Knock!
Who's there?
Duck.
Duck who?
Duck!
A baseball is about to hit your door.

Knock Knock!
Who's there?
Hen.
Hen who?
Hen are you going to open the door?

Knock Knock!
Who's there?
Sheep.
Sheep who?
Sheep will be sailing in a moment – hurry up!

Knock Knock!
Who's there?
Tuna.
Tuna who?
Tuna toothpaste!

Knock Knock!
Who's there?
Bull.
Bull who?
Bull the chain.

Knock Knock!
Who's there?
Toad.
Toad who?
Toad you I was coming round.

Knock Knock!
Who's there?
Shark.
Shark who?
Shark horror!
I thought there was no one in!

Knock Knock!
Who's there?
Whale.
Whale who?
Whale wait outside if you like.

Knock Knock!
Who's there?
Moose.
Moose who?
Moose polite people would open the door.

Knock Knock!
Who's there?
Ram.
Ram who?
Rambo of course!

Knock Knock!
Who's there?
Prawn.
Prawn who?
Prawn a pretty dress – we're going dancing.

Did you hear?

Have you got your ear to the ground? Of course you haven't – it would be all messy and full of soil if you had. But listen up! We've heard lots of things about some animal quackers and we thought it only fair to tell you.

Have you heard about the boy who does bird impressions?
He eats worms.

Did you hear about the cricket team who had a kangaroo for a bowler?
He bowled long hops.

Did you hear about the bull that got into a china shop?
It had a smashing time.

Did you hear about the raven who joined the police force?
They called him a rookie.

Did you hear about the people who were eaten alive in London in the 1960s?
They went into Lion's Coffee House.

Did you hear about the dog who was called Johann Sebastian?
There was something wrong with his Bach.

Did you hear about the dog who ate his owner's dictionary?
His owner took the words right out of his mouth.

Did you hear about the poor man who always bought chicken to eat?
It cost a poultry sum.

Did you hear about the chicken who got married?
She went to a hen party.

Did you hear about the blackbird who joined a pop group?
They said, "He's raven again."

Did you hear about the sheepdog trials?
Four were found guilty as charged.

Did you hear about the short-sighted turtle?
He fell in love with an army helmet and died of a
broken heart.

Did you hear about the donkey with an IQ of 175?
Nobody liked him because he was such a smart-ass.

$$\frac{x}{y} > 9.23 \left(\frac{x^2}{y} \times Q \right)^2$$

Did you hear about the stupid farmer who was killed
by a cow?
It fell on him while he was having a drink.

Did you hear about the trainee woodpecker?
It was learning the drill.

Did you hear about the man who wanted to buy a parrot?
He didn't have enough money so he bought a bird that was going cheap.

Did you hear about the musical shark?
He had sharp teeth.

Did you hear about the shark called Robin Hood?
He robbed the rich poises to feed the porpoises.

Did you hear about the mean man who went to the pet shop for a black and white dog?
He thought the license would be cheaper.

Did you hear about the tiger that ate Aesop?
He said, "Now try making a fable out of that one."

Did you hear about the lion who became a cannibal?
He had to swallow his pride.

Did you hear about the cat that fell in the yoghurt?
She's a sour puss now.

Did you hear about the fight in the fish shop?
All the fish got battered.

Did you hear about the stupid water polo player?
The horse drowned.

Did you hear about the frog who set up a flower shop?
What did he sell?
Croakuses.

Did you hear of the bull who swallowed a bomb?
He was a-bomb-in-a-bull.

Did you hear about the bull called Terry?
He was Terry-bul.

Did you hear about the silly girl who found some milk bottles in a field?
She thought she'd found a cow's nest.

Did you hear the joke about the lion?
No.
When you hear it you will roar.

Did you hear about the chicken that fell into the cement mixer?
She became a bricklayer.

Did you hear about the man who opened a betting shop in a field?
He said, "That'll get the sheep gambolling."

Did you hear about the cowardly canary?
He was yellow.

Did you hear about the mole who ate three tins of
baked beans?
He got wind in the willows.

Did you hear about the fisherman who caught a trout
and a grillfer?
What's a grillfer?
To cook fish under.

Did you hear about the battery hen?
It laid electric eggs.

Did you hear about the man who took his dog to obedience school?
The dog passed but he failed.

Did you hear about the hyena who swallowed an Oxo cube?
He made a real laughing stock of himself.

Did you hear about the fish that swims backwards?
It helps keep the water out of its eyes.

Did you hear about the drunken snail?
He had to go over a five-bar gate.

Animal
Insults

Are you fed up with rude remarks from your classmates? Well learn some of these and you will be able to come back at them with some stinging lines that have more bite than a crocodile who's just had his teeth sharpened.

If your brain were a Great Dane it could only hold one flea at a time!

You have the brain of a jackass.
I know, when do you want it back?

You're so stupid, if I called you a birdbrain I'd be giving you a compliment.

I know we all originally spring from animals but you didn't spring far enough.

If I had to sit next to you in class I'd put a tiger in your desk.
If I had to sit next to *you* in class I'd let it eat me.

I hung a picture of you in my basement to scare the rats away.
Well I hung a picture of you in my basement and it killed the rats – they died laughing.

You look familiar. Haven't I seen you in a wildlife documentary?
No, you probably saw me in the bush – I was the one filming you.

You look familiar, but then that's
understandable – I collect reptiles as a hobby.

You look familiar. Didn't I dissect you in a
biology class?

You eat like a bird – a vulture.

You eat like a bird too – but that's OK if you *like*
worms.

You're so ugly a hippopotamus would beat you in a beauty contest.

You have a distinctive laugh – but then so does a hyena.

Your family is so mad, when the clock goes "cuckoo, cuckoo" they all take it personally.

I like the perfume you're wearing – "Night At The Zoo."

Just because you smell like an ape, doesn't mean you're Tarzan.

I change my underwear as often as you clean your cage.

When you go to the zoo, the monkeys put on gas masks.

I won't be angry with you today – it's "Be Kind to Animals Week."

You have the memory of an elephant – and the face to go with it.

You can't go for a long walk – your lead doesn't stretch that far.

I say, I say, I say...

What's brown, burrows underground and is made of cement?
I don't know, what is it?
A mole – the cement was just to make it hard.

Why are all cowboys bow-legged?
They can't get their calves together.

Look, the pelican's just stuck her head in the wall socket.
What did she do that for?
To get an electric bill.

Did you hear about the lion tamer who'd had a nasty accident?
No, what was his name?
Claud Bottom.

My sister's just been swallowed by a lion.
Oh, she must be down in the mouth.

Why is your dog called Carpenter?
Because he does little jobs around the house.

That cow makes it's own butter.
That's impossible.
No – she's got hiccoughs.

Some cows have been stolen!
It must have been a beef burglar.

How can you get milk from a cat?
Steal her saucer.

I can speak to animals you know.
Good, next time you see a skunk ask him what's his reason for living.

We really love our dog. He's just like one of the family.
Really? Which one?

Does your dog bite strangers?
Only ones he doesn't know.

I've started putting clothes on my pig.
Really, why?
I'm fed up with streaky bacon.

My dad's going to buy a Jaguar.
You'd better watch it. Those things bite.

You: "Isn't it lucky to have a black cat following you?"
Me: "That depends on whether you're a man or a mouse."

You: "Our cat has good breeding."
Me: "I know, she's had 10 kittens already."

What's yellow and smells of bananas?
Don't tell me – the monkey's been sick again.

What has four legs and flies?
Don't tell me – the horse is dirty again.

I like to keep my pig under the bed.
What about the smell?
Oh, he doesn't mind that.

I call my dog Ironmonger.
Why is that?
Because whenever someone comes to the door the
dog makes a bolt for it.

I call my dog Boxer.
Why is that?
Because whenever the doorbell rings the dog runs
into the corner.

Our cat got first prize in the budgie show.
That's impossible, cats don't get prizes in budgie
shows.
Ours did. The budgie got the first prize and our cat
got the budgie.

There's a black cat in the kitchen.
So? Black cats are lucky.
This one certainly is. It's just eaten your dinner.

Our dog's in the police force.
He doesn't look like a police dog.
That's because he's in the secret police.

See this fur, it comes from the grizzly bear.
I didn't know you got fur from a grizzly.
You do, as fur as you possibly can.

I think there's a pickpocket about.
Why do you say that?
Because the kangaroo's just lost its baby.

1st fisherman: "How are the fish today?"
2nd fisherman: "I don't know, I haven't dropped them
a line yet."

When I was at school I was the teacher's pet.
Why?
She couldn't afford a dog.

We've taught one of our chickens to box.
Has it won anything?
Yes, the bantamweight.

Our dog doesn't eat any meat?
Really? Why's that?
We don't give him any.

Does your dog have a family tree?
No, he doesn't mind which tree he uses.

Anyone seen the dog bowl?
No, but I've seen him make some pretty good
catches.

Have you ever seen a catfish?
Yes, but it beats me how they can hold the rod.

Is it good manners to eat chicken with your fingers?
No, you should eat them separately.

Customer: "I'd like a pair of crocodile boots please."
Assistant: "Certainly, what size is your crocodile?"

What do you call a coward in a boat?
Chicken of the Sea.

I just got a pair of alligator shoes. It took me ages to get them off the alligator!

If a camel can go for 500 miles without water, how long could it go *with* water?

How long can a goose stand on one leg?
I don't know.
Well try it and see.

If cowboys ride horses, what do you call someone who rides cows?
Weird.

Have you put the cat out?
I didn't know it was on fire!

Why did the shark not attack the woman who fell overboard?
Because it was a man-eating shark.

One of my fish is very upset. He's tried everything and he still can't earn any money.
Poor sole.

Oh, give me a home where the buffalo roam...
...and I'll show you a house with very dirty carpets!

You: "Do you know how long dogs should be bathed?"
Me: "The same time as short ones."

You: "My cat's covered in ticks."
Me: "Well you shouldn't have wound him up so much."

Has your cat ever had fleas?
No, just kittens.

When I was in the jungle the trees were full of these big white animals.
What were they?
Lost polar bears.

See that cat? It has drunk **74** saucers of milk without stopping.
That must be a lap record.

Did you know it takes a dozen sheep to make a sweater?
Really? I didn't know they could knit.

Why do you call your tadpole "Tiny"?
Because he's my newt.

Don't go out in the kitchen, King Kong's out there.
He sounds dangerous.
Yes, don't monkey with him.

1st pig: "What are you eating?"
2nd pig: "Not telling, nosey porker!"

My brother put our budgie in the washing machine.
That must have killed it.
No, but the tumble drier did.

Your dog's been chasing a man on a bicycle.
Don't be silly, my dog can't ride a bicycle.

All my clothes smell of fish?
Why is that?
Because I'm a dab hand at ironing.

I call my dog Isaiah.
Why do you call him Isaiah?
Because one eye's higher than the other.

I take my dog for a tramp in the woods every day.
Does your dog enjoy it?
Yes, but the tramp's getting a little fed up.

I shot my dog yesterday?
Was he mad?
Well, he wasn't exactly happy about it.

You: "Can you sing any of the songs from 'Cats'?"
Me: "No, none of my cats could ever sing."

You: "Have you ever seen a fox trot?"
Me: "No, but I've seen a cat nap."

Will you put some fresh water in the goldfish bowl?
What's the point? He hasn't drunk the last lot yet!

What family does the aardvark belong to?
I didn't know anyone in the street had one.

Elephant: "I'm sorry, but I can't pay my bill."
Hotel manager: "In that case you can pack your trunk
and go."

How do you get down off a giraffe?
You don't, you get down off a goose.

Teacher: "Why is there a hyphen in 'bird-cage'?"
Pupil: "So that the bird has something to sit on, Miss.

Have you got any kittens going cheap?
No sir, all our kittens go miaow.

I used to think I was a dog but the psychiatrist cured me.
Are you sure?
Oh yes, feel my paw and see how firm it is.

Did you hear about Jonah who fell into the sea and
was swallowed by an enormous fish?
No what happened to him?
He had a whale of a time.

Fifty pedigree dogs were stolen from Cruft's Dog
Show yesterday. Police say they have no leads.

If your cat swallows a coin does that mean you've got
money in the kitty?

What did you do on Sunday?
Went riding.
Horseback?
Oh yes, he got back an hour before I did.

Do you sell horses meat?
Only if they're accompanied by their owners.

Have you ever noticed that a dog hates it if you blow
in his face but if you take them in the car they will
stick their head out of the window?

My dog has no nose.
How does he smell?
Terrible.

You: "Why do you call your dog 'Camera'?"
Me: "Because he's always snapping."

Teacher: "Which poet wrote 'To a Nightingale'?"
Pupil: "Whoever it was, I bet he didn't get a reply."

You: "Name four cats in the cat family."
Me: "Mummy cat, daddy cat and the two kittens."

Customer: "Have you got anything to cure fleas on my dog?"
Pet shop owner: "I don't know. What's wrong with them?"

Me: "Our cat can play chess you know."
You: "Really? She must be very clever."
Me: "I suppose so except I'm beating her three games to two."

Stories

An enormous lion was prowling proudly through the jungle one day when he came across a zebra. "Who's the King of the Jungle?" asked the lion. "You are," replied the zebra timidly. Later he met a monkey. "Who's the King of the Jungle?" he asked. "You are," replied the monkey. Then he saw an elephant walking through the undergrowth. "Elephant," growled the lion, "who is King of the Jungle?" Suddenly the elephant picked the lion up with his trunk and threw him against a tree. He then swung him around three times in a circle and hurled him into the nearest lake. "All right," grumbled the miserable, battered lion, "just because you don't know the answer there's no need to get angry."

Two hundred dairy cows slipped and fell over today as they were herded along an icy country lane. A spokesperson for the Farmers' Association said that the incident was unfortunate, but added that it was no use crying over spilt milk.

A boy went to the doctor with an elephant on his head. The doctor said "My word, you don't half need help." The elephant said, "I'll say I do. Get this kid out from under me."

An elephant met a mouse in the jungle. "Gosh you're small," said the elephant to the mouse. "Yes I know," replied the mouse, "I haven't been well."

A man went to the butchers and said, "I'd like some bits for the dog, please." The butcher said, "Certainly, which bits are missing?"

A sick kangaroo went to a hospital and started banging on the door. "What do you want?" the doctor said. The kangaroo replied, "a hoperation." The doctor said, "So what do you think is wrong with you?" The kangaroo said, "I've been run over and I've broken both my legs." The doctor said, "Well I'm sorry to have to tell you that that is an in-hop-erable condition."

Two hunters were arguing about some tracks they found while hunting. "They're lion tracks," said one. "No, they're bear tracks," said the other. While they were arguing a train ran over them.

A girl was walking down the road with an ugly, miserable-looking turkey under her arm. "Where did you get it?" asked a passer-by. "I won her at a raffle," replied the turkey.

A boy and his girlfriend were walking through a field. "Ah, look at that cow and calf rubbing noses," said the boy, "it makes me want to do the same." "Well go ahead," said the girl, "it's your cow."

A stupid woman went into a pet shop for some birdseed. "What kind would you like?" asked the shop assistant. "Well I don't know," replied the woman, "which ones grow the fastest?"

A mother bird was very upset and flying round her nest. "What's the matter?" said a passing owl. "It's my baby bird," she said, "he's about to fall out of the nest." "Quick" said the owl, "we'll get him a sparrow-chute."

There were three fishermen in a boat. Two of them started shouting "Killer whale! Killer whale!" The third man looked irritated and replied, "Look, I don't know how to kill a whale, all right!"

A lion tamer in a circus liked to live in his lions' cages. "I don't mind him doing it," said his boss to a visitor, "he's 'armless enough."

A baby polar bear was sitting on an iceberg with his mother. "Mommie," he said, "am I a real polar bear?" "Of course you are, dear," she replied. "Really, really a polar bear?" "Yes dear, you're a real polar bear," said his mother. "And you're sure I'm not any other kind of bear," he added. "Of course, you're not. Why do you ask?" she said. "Because I'm freezing!" he replied.

A great game hunter was telling his friends of his recent exploits in the jungle. "See that lion in the glass case," he said, "well, I shot that lion in Africa where I was on safari with my wife Janet." "Is it stuffed?" asked one of them. "Yes," he replied, "with my wife Janet."

Two cows told the farmer that they wanted to write to each other. "Don't be silly," said the farmer, "you're in the same pen." "I know," replied one of the cows, "but we want to be pen friends."

A baby giraffe ran up to his mother and said, "Mommie, Mommie, I've got wet feet. Do you think I'll get a sore throat?" "Yes," replied his mother, "but not until next week.

A donkey was boasting to his friends in the farmyard. He said, "If I were tied to a rope six feet long and there was a bale of hay eighteen feet away from me, I could still get to eat that hay." "No you couldn't," said the other animals, "you're just boasting. How could you do it?" "I'd make sure the six-foot rope wasn't tied to anything else," replied the donkey.

There was a football match and one of the teams turned up with 10 men and a chicken. "Sorry," said the referee, "I can't let your team play." "Why not?" said the team captain. "Because," he replied, "I don't allow foul play."

A man knocked on an old lady's door and said, "I'm awfully sorry but I've just run over your cat. To make it up to you, though, I'll happily replace it." "Really," replied the old lady, "can you catch mice?"

A man went to the doctors and said "I've just been shot by a duck." "Don't be silly," said the doctor, "ducks can't shoot." "This one could," he replied, "I shot at it and it shot back at me. It was a quack shot."

A man bought a parrot and the shop assistant told him "I guarantee you that this bird will repeat every word he hears." After three days the man brought the bird back. "He hasn't said a word since I've had him," he complained. The shop assistant replied, "That's because he's deaf."

There were two farmers who each had a horse in the same field. In order to tell them apart they had a little rubber band round one of the horse's tails. Every day they used to come down to the field and feel up and down the horses' tails until they found the rubber band. Then one day they lost it and didn't know what to do. Then one farmer said to the other, "I know what we'll do. I'll have the black horse and you have the white one."

A farmer went to the vet and said "I've got a terrible problem. One of my cows has just swallowed my entire stereo system." The vet said, "What, the loudspeakers as well?" "Yes, the loudspeakers as well," said the farmer. "In that case," said the vet, "I think we're going to get some feedback."

A couple of goats were eating some old reels of film outside a cinema. "What are you eating?" said one to the other. "Gone with the Wind," he replied. "Is it good?" asked the first one. "It's OK," he replied, "but I preferred the book."

A burglar broke into a man's house. Suddenly he was attacked by the man's dog who hung onto his legs with his very sharp teeth. "Please, please call your dog off," pleaded the burglar. "I can't," said the man, "he's used to me calling him Buster."

A man found a chimpanzee sitting on his garden wall so he rang up the police and said, "What shall I do with him?" The police said, "Take him to the zoo at once." The next day he rang the police again and said, "He likes the zoo very much. Got any more ideas?"

A boy went to work for a zoo vet. "Look in the lion's mouth," the vet told him. "How do I do that?" he said. "Carefully," replied the vet.

A fisherman caught a little herring. "You don't want me," said the herring, "I've got a lot of bad habits." "That's all right," said the fisherman, "I'll cure you."

A man was out hunting when two ducks swam past going "Quack, quack." "Shut up," he said, "I'm going as quack as I can."

A little sheep wanted to be let into the farmhouse because of the rain. It stood outside going "Baa, baa," but the farmer was hard hearted and shouted, "Go away. Don't be such a wet blanket."

A man went into a pet shop to complain. "You sold me a canary with a broken leg," he said. "Well, you said you wanted a bird that could sing," replied the shopkeeper, "you didn't say you wanted it to dance as well."

An elephant and a mouse were playing in opposing football teams and the mouse had the ball. He was about to score when all of a sudden the elephant lifted up his foot and squashed him flat. The referee said, "That's a foul. That's a sending off offence. What do you think you're doing?" The elephant said "Nothing! I was only trying to trip him up!"

Hickory, dickory, dock. The mice ran up the clock. The clock struck one, so all the others ran away.

A man wanted to buy a dog from the Dog's Home but he didn't know where it was. He went to a big building which he thought was the Home and knocked on the door. A woman opened the door and the man said, "Dog's Home?" "I don't know," she replied, then she shouted indoors, "Rex, you in?...."

A man went into a pet shop and said, "How much is that cockatoo?" The shopkeeper said, "A reasonable price." The man said, "All right, send me the bill." The shopkeeper said, "I'm sorry sir, it's the whole bird or nothing."

When God made all the animals they held a raffle to see who would get what. The lion got a mane, the leopard got spots, the cat got a miaow and so on. Then at the end God came round to say goodbye and all the animals lined up to shake his hand. Then God said, "Where's the camel? The camel's not here to say goodbye." And St Peter said, "The camel's not coming. He's got the hump."

Two elephants were fighting over who should go into the swimming pool first. A mouse was watching nearby and said, "Why are you fighting? Can't you just go into the pool together." "No," they replied, "we've only got one pair of trunks between us."

A man was driving along a country road when he saw a miserable-looking hitch-hiking frog. The man stopped and said "What's the matter?" "I'm un-hoppy," said the frog. "Do you want a lift then?" said the man. "Yes please," said the frog. "OK," said the man, "hop in."

Limericks

I once had a parrot named Polly
Who flew down and bit my ice lolly.
She broke off her beak
So now she can't speak
And there's no more lolly for Polly.

There once was a hamster called Larry
Who decided he wanted to marry.
So he changed his whole life
And looked for a wife
And that was the end of old Larry.

There once was a pony called Jake
Who, sadly, was thin as a rake.
He refused all his dinner
Got thinner and thinner
Till just one last gasp he could take.

There once was a very strong cat
Who had a fight with a little black bat
The bat flew away
And by the end of the day
The cat had a scrap with a rat.

The angora goat's very hairy
So you must be exceedingly wary
For when the wind blows
The fluff tickles his nose
And his sneezing becomes almost scary.

There once was an old billy goat
With a ball-bearing stuck in his throat.
He coughed and he spluttered
And in anguish he muttered
From now on I'll just stick to oats.

A billy goat with horns spectacular
Whose curves were impressively circular
Once charged at a log
Which he thought was a dog
Now his horns are oddly triangular.

There once was a rabbit named Buster
Who I mistook for a feather duster.
I polished a chair
And now I don't dare
To tell you what happened to Buster.

There once was a pony called Matt
Who was exceedingly fat
With a tumble and sneeze
He fell on his knees
And that was the end of poor Matt.

A warthog who thought herself plain
Tried to dress herself up, but in vain
For her ringlets and spangles
And an earring that dangles
Have been utterly ruined by rain.

A toucan made other birds shriek
By pinching their toes with her beak
But she then bit the claws
Of a bird with large jaws
And then tweaked nothing more for a week.

A musical squid learned the flute
And could rattle a drum with one foot
Then he practised all day
And was able to play
The piano, guitar and the lute.

An inquisitive moose strayed too near
An adventurous young pioneer
So this gigantic beast
Made a wonderful feast
And his antlers a fine chandelier.

There was a young man of Bengal
Who was asked to a fancy dress ball
He said he would risk it
He went as a biscuit
But a dog ate him up in the hall.

There was a young lady with vigor
Who rode with a smile on a tiger
They returned from the ride
With the lady inside
And the smile on the face of the tiger.

An elephant from hilly Tibet
In his cage one day wouldn't get
So his keeper quite near
Rammed a hose in his rear
And invented the first jumbo jet.

A young man who's as bald as a bat
Spilt hair tonic over the mat
It's grown so much higher
We can't see the fire
And we think it's smothered the cat.

Further Reading

How to Feed Elephants by P. Nutts.
The Joys of Horse Riding by Jim Karna.
The Escape of the Elephant by Gay Topen.
I've Been Bitten! by A. Flea.
The Lion Tamer by Claudia Armoff.
House Train Your Cat by Phil D. Littreboxx.
House Train Your Dog by Hope N. Deedore.
Cleaning Your Doberman's Teeth by Hugo First.
How to Break Up a Fight Between Two Dogs by Luke Out.
Escape a Charging Rhino by Ron N. Hyde.
Escape a Charging Bull by Clem. A. Tree.
Will the Lion Catch the Zebra? by Betty Will.
How Much does a Baby Elephant Eat? by A. Lot.
How Much Does a Fully Grown Elephant Eat by Men E. More.
The Dog That Howls All Night by Major Headache.
The Tiger is Loose by R. U. Scared.
Would You Like a Puppy for Christmas? by Felix Ited.
Animals from The South Pole by Ann Tartic.
How I Crossed the Desert by Rhoda Camul.
How to Stop a Charging Elephant by Dinah Mite.
How to Feed Your Rabbit by Rosa Carrots.
Outsize Clothes by Ellie Fant.
Feed the Dog a Bone by Ivor Chew.
What Do Bats See? by I. C. Stars.
Eating Habits of the Pig by R. E. Volting.